EMPATH: WHY YOUR INTUITION MATTERS AND WHAT YOUR BODY IS TELLING YOU

Empaths Survival with 17 Habits to Ensure Survival

Frank Knoll

Disclaimer:

Table of Contents

Introduction

If you are highly sensitive and you feel connected with the energy around you, you are an empath. Do not be afraid of your inherent ability and gifts. You are here on Earth to serve a purpose. With your genuine caring nature, you can soothe the pains of others. You can enhance the vibration of a room with your positive energy. You can heal yourself and other people. Another book that has been helpful in our knowledge to discover ourselves is <u>Psychic Empath</u>, which helps to better understand what an Empath is, and how to understand yourself.

However, you can also absorb the negativity in your surroundings which can make you emotionally drained. In this state, you cannot serve your purpose well. There is a need to recharge, rejuvenate, and release the excess energy inside your body.

This book is here to guide you toward empowerment. It will discuss why your intuition is vital and how it will help you in your empath journey. Your body takes the toll of excessive energy and negative emotions, so you need to listen to it.

Section 1 helps you understand the world of an empath and the importance of intuition for you.

Chapter 1 introduces the types of empaths and the role of intuition for them.

Chapter 2 provides steps, so you can understand how your body and your intuition heals.

Chapter 3 gives you strategies to protect and heal yourself using intuition when illness strikes.

Chapter 4 helps you understand your emotions by focusing on the light, guarding against negativity, and practicing affirmations.

Chapter 5 presents the concept of healing, using sexual energy.

Section 2 lists 17 survival tips for empaths.

Section 1

Chapter 1

Empath Overview and What is Intuition Relating to an Empath

Empaths are hypersensitive individuals with high levels of understanding and compassion for the emotions of other people. They connect with others in a deeper sense and are often known to actually "feel" their emotions.

However, many born empaths are not aware of this fact. They believe that what is happening to them is normal and simply accepted the fact that they are sensitive.

The world is full of empaths. People label them as sensitive. Most of them are artists, singers, or writers. Because of their sensitivity, empaths become poets in motion. They are also very interested in different cultures and view them with a wider perspective.

They are everywhere. They could be anyone among your family, colleagues, peers, friends, or workmates.

Empaths are the world's greatest listeners. Most often, they are the thinkers, the learners, or the problem solvers. Their deep comprehension and understanding of things make them the "wind beneath the wings" of people in their life. For empaths, every problem has an answer and they are always ready to look for one.

6 Types of Empaths

Emotional Empath

This type is the most common kind of empath. If you are an emotional empath, you are easily affected by the prevailing emotions of people around you. Without even trying to, you pick them up and feel the impact of those emotions like you are the one dealing with the issue.

You feel a sudden sadness in the middle of a crowd even if you are not sad. You may feel angry for no reason at all. You feel panicky and troubled while being puzzled, because you have no reason to feel that way at all. These unexpected barrages of emotions are not yours, they are from individuals around you.

It is vital to know your own emotions and know when you are picking up another person's emotions. This will help you protect yourself and enable you to help other people without the risk of being emotionally drained.

Physical or Medical Empath

This person easily picks up the dominant energy in the bodies of other people. Physical or medical empaths intuitively know the cause of illness of another person. They would instantly feel "an awareness" inside their own body when treating or touching other people. Individuals in this classification usually become healers. Some pursue the medical profession, while others prefer to practice alternative healing methods.

You should learn to differentiate whether the symptom that you feel is yours or not. Awareness is important because if you accept it as yours, it may eventually cause you real illness.

Intuitive or Claircognizant Empath

Do you easily pick up information or connect with other people's mental thoughts when you are around them? Do you sometimes wonder why you seem to know the person by just glancing at him?

If you relate to any of the above, you are a claircognizant or intuitive empath. You know when someone is lying or hiding something from you. You can immediately sense the intention of another person through the words they say. This is a rare gift, which connects you with the energy of another individual and gives you the ability to read it to decipher their intentions, emotions, and thoughts.

You need a strong energetic field to protect yourself from non-stop bombardment of energies from your surroundings. Align yourself also with other gifted individuals who can help you maximize your intuitive power.

Geomantic Empath

You are a geomantic empath if you're deeply attuned to the environment or physical landscape. Some places make you feel good and happy while you feel a sudden discomfort or overwhelming fear without apparent reason in other places.

This deep connection in certain places is the main characteristic of a highly-geomantic empath. Some are drawn into sacred places like churches, groves, and sacred stones. Others want to be around historical places like museums. You are also sensitive to the damages that occur in the natural world and you grieve for them.

As a geomantic empath, your energy is easily recharged when you spend time communing with nature. Your spirit soars when your environment has natural scents, plants, and other things that remind you of nature.

Animal Empath

The person who intuitively knows what animals need, is an animal empath. There is a mysterious connection between them and these creatures. If you love animals and you are very much interested in nurturing them, then you belong to this empath category.

You can become an animal healer. Your natural instinct to understand them is your best tool to help animals who need tender care and assistance.

Plant Empath

You are a plant empath if you intuitively know the needs of plants. You know where to find the ideal place for them in the garden or even inside your home. If your job is related to plants, then you have found your niche. You gift belongs to the kingdom of flora where you can offer your skill to nurture them. Some plant empaths even claimed that the trees and plants are guiding them.

The Role of Intuition

Empaths of any kind are highly intuitive people. Their intuition is deeply attuned to the object of their attention, whether they are aware of it or not.

Chapter 2
Understanding Your Body

Healing is about the restoration of health and well-being. There are many ancient healing practices that are still used today - from traditional to alternative forms. All of them claim to be the best option for any type of disease that you may have.

However, there is another method that is becoming popular: intuition healing.

Understanding Intuition Healing

Intuition lives inside your body. It is deeply rooted in your biological components. It is intrinsically connected with the Divine Power or the Source, so you can never go wrong with using it.

The healing intuition basically connects your body and mind. It is the increased sensitivity and awareness of your body's changing condition. With it, you can easily understand your health issues, learn how to nurture yourself, and heal the underlying causes.

It is your master guide to complete healing and well-being. Your intuitive intelligence is your secret asset to healing yourself and others. You can heal yourself alone or you can connect with others who are well-equipped with the knowledge and skills in intuitive healing.

When you fully understand how intuition healing operates, you have in your hand the greatest power to heal. It all begins with the awakening of the dormant skill which is always inside of you.

Steps to Understanding

Step 1: Find out if you are an intuitive healer through these telltale signs:

1. **You are intuitive.** You instinctively know how things will unfold. People come to you when they have problems and you easily anticipate what they want or need.

You often have visions and vivid dreams of what will occur even before it happens.

2. **You are sensitive.** You are easily overwhelmed by the rush, noise, and arguments in the environment. You are extremely sensitive to energies that people emit based upon their emotional state. You prefer calm, quiet, and peaceful spaces.

3. **You have a big and compassionate heart.** You sense others' pains and fears. People who want to feel better seek your company. They feel safe telling their deep secrets with you.

4. **You like being alone**. By nature, you are an introvert. You prefer to be alone to balance and restore your spent energy. Large crowds overwhelm and drain you.

5. **You enjoy helping other people**. You find meaning and enjoyment when you help others. Or, perhaps, you are already helping them as a doctor, nurse, therapist, counselor, or therapist.

6. **You are attracted to healing**. It excites you. You want to learn more about healing and explore it. You know that it is your calling.

7. **You are aware of energy**. You sense both positive and negative energies. You have a deep understanding of the world, the situations that occur and the experiences that you are having.

Step 2: Listen to your inner wisdom.

The quiet voice in your head that speaks to you is your intuition. It comes in dreams, visions, gut feelings, memories, hunches, physical sensations, or urgent appeals that you clearly hear in a flash.

Step 3: Trust Your Intuition

Your soul or your Higher Self speaks through your intuition. You need to trust it and allow it to guide you through life.

You need to understand that the physical manifestations are directly connected with your thoughts and emotions. To seek the power of your higher vibrations and create a healthier physical life, it is important to develop your intuitive intelligence.

Step 4: Strengthen your intuition.

1. **Create space.** If you are keen on developing the intuition, you need to dedicate a regular time for it. Practice yoga or meditation to open your Ajna chakra or the third eye.

2. **Practice gratitude.** Practice giving thanks to people, situation, manifestation, and confirmation that come your way. It attracts a perpetual cycle of positive growth and success. It also fosters better relationships.

3. **Look, feel, and listen.** Whenever you are alone, allow your mind to be quiet. Stop thinking about your problems, your fears, and other mundane tasks. This is the time of allowing. Let messages come into your mind without attaching too much to them. Let it come and go. Keep

your mind open until you hear significant messages that you know come from the Higher Power.

4. **Be creative.** Honor your intuition by documenting your progress and expressing them through writings, dancing, singing, drawing, and other creative means.

5. **Trust yourself.** Intuition is the voice that helps you make quick decisions when it comes to any situation or dilemma that you encounter. It comes when you do not know which way to go. Your intuitive gift is connected to the Divine Intelligence and it's got you covered at all times, so long as you listen to it.

Chapter 3
How to Use Intuition to Heal Yourself?

Your body is the physical manifestation of energies. Your every choice has a consequence that affects your health positively or negatively. When you are aware of this, you know that everything happens at the energetic level.

When illness strikes, you can turn into your intuitive power to heal yourself.

Various Ways to Heal Yourself Using Intuition:

Insight Healing

This alternative healing method uses the five senses to locate, correct, and eliminate the imbalances of energy in the body. The key components are focused-thinking and visualization.

- With the help of a skilled practitioner, you will be assisted in visualizing an energy blockage and the process of breaking it down. You can visualize it being dismantled by pieces or melting it down with a healing light. Whichever you choose, the final image that you will visualize is a clean, clear, and healthy organ.

Activate Your Intuition to Heal Yourself

- Meditate to control your thoughts. You need to dispel self-destructive and negative thoughts with positive ones. Attune yourself to higher frequency energy, such as positive, loving, and healing thoughts.

- Next, focus on your emotions. Let them come out without attaching yourself or denying them. Just allow them to pass without judging or criticizing. Release them all.

- Finally, visualize yourself in a healthy state physically, mentally, emotionally, and spiritually. See yourself in perfect health through your mind's eye.

Practice this intuition healing method every time you feel sick, weak, or drained. Knowing how easy to use intuitive healing, you can improve your well-being and health from the inside out.

Tap Your Inner Guidance

- Inhale deeply and center yourself. Bring your focus and attention to your heart area where wisdom and power converges. There is a connecting vein that connects the heart and the brain. Your heart processes the information intuitively and sends it to the brain.

- Once you connect with your heart, begin to ask yourself with questions that require a "yes or no" answers. For example, "Will it be beneficial to me if I use this supplement?"

- Wait for the answer. The answer must come from the heart and not from the brain. Take note of how your heart answers you. It may come as a spreading of warmth in the heart zone or a sense of lightness. It can be a slight pain or a constriction of the heart. Pay attention to know the right answer.

- Once you have the answer, acknowledge your heart's wisdom by saying thank you to it.

Engage in activities which you intuitively feel are good and beneficial to you.

- Stop doing other things that stress you out. Anything that gives a feeling of goodness produces a higher energy vibration and promotes the healing process. The opposite will make you sick and weak.

When your intuition keeps nagging on a health issue, listen.

- Check the information pertaining to the issue.

- Consult a doctor and let him examine your body.

Tap into your intuition as you research for the best health provider or therapist.

- Attune yourself to your body and heart wisdom.

- Study each option and allow your intuition to help you decide.

Respond early to your intuition's call.

- Listen to your intuition.

- Respond and act immediately on the clues in your physical body to prevent, reduce, or halt the progress of any disease.

When your intuition keeps nagging you, allow it to show you the details.

- Stop discerning the specifics.

- Surrender yourself to the meaning of its advice.

Chapter 4
Understanding Your Emotions

The outstanding trademark of empaths is their high-sensitivity to other people's emotions. The downside of this ability is that they can also easily absorb these energies and physical symptoms, which can affect them negatively. This is the challenge that every empath faces in their lifetime.

Therefore, it is necessary to guard yourself at all times to prevent the negative energies to sap your positive energy.

Here are three ways to keep your energy positive:

Focusing on the light.

As an empath, your light shines brightly when you are centered and balanced. You are full of love and positive energy. You light up the world with your own unique personality. You may be a little laid-back but your capacity to listen, to nurture, to empathize, and to help other people make you a shining light amidst a challenging life.

Keeping the light on is your greatest battle. As an empath, you are easily affected by strong emotions that surround you. To maintain your positivity, always follow or do what lights you up. If you love singing, sing. If you love writing, write a blog. If you love dancing, go for it. Anything that makes you feel good will help in keeping the light on.

Flood yourself with the positive energy brought by this light every moment of the day. It includes physical light, spiritual light, and emotional experiences that are full of light.

Pray daily. Surround yourself with happiness. Breathe fresh air.

Bring light into your home. Light up the dark areas. Bring fresh flowers and plants. Regenerate the physical space around you. Bring life inside to nurture your spirit.

Guarding against negativity.
You are like a sponge who absorbs the dominant emotions of people or energy of

objects around you. Here are effective ways to guard yourself against these negative energies.

- *Create strong boundaries*

   To stop yourself from suffering from the stress that you absorb in your noisy or crowded surroundings, learn to detach. The best protection you can give to yourself is prevention. Stop trying to fix everything for others and help them when they are prepared to be helped.

   You can surround yourself with small psychological barriers like a plant, pet photo, or family photo. Anything that makes you feel positive. Sacred objects also help such as crystals, protective stones, sacred beads, rosary, the Buddha, or statue of Quan Yin (goddess of compassion).

   Music that relaxes you or lifts your spirit is also beneficial.

- *Beware of energy vampires*

These are the people in your life that suck and drain your positive energy. You'll always feel exhausted after spending time with them. Most of them ask for sympathy and love in a demanding way. They keep on relating their sob stories again and again, and then expect your total attention.

Other energy vampires are those who are jealous of you and unconsciously send negative energies. Take note that an emotionally charged intention is very powerful, so it is best to steer clear of them.

Shield or ground yourself before spending time with these kinds of people. Keep a firm boundary and make it short.

Another method of protection is to imagine yourself inside a big, clear bubble which repels negative energy.

- *Wear protective gemstones or crystals*

Quartz and other crystals are used since

time immemorial for protection. Choose one that will specifically ward off negative energies. You can also wear gemstones that attract positive energies to empower yourself against negative forces in the environment.

- *Meditate*

  Meditation helps you balance the energy in your body. It centers you and dispels the accumulated negative energies inside you. Find a meditation practice that helps you become more empowered. Try chakra meditation to help you clean your energy points in the body.

  Practice it regularly to sustain your connection with your Higher Self.

- *Water*

  Water purification is used by many cultures around the globe. Water represents a flowing energy of Earth that washes off negative energies.

Take a shower with water infused with your intention to wash away the negative energies in your body. Imagine yourself in a waterfall and let the water remove any dark energy from within.

- *Make a Journal*

Making journal is one effective way to release stagnant energy. You can write everything down in your journal, even the most embarrassing experiences.

See how your emotions change as you jot down your anger, sadness, frustration, and other negative feelings. As you keep writing, your energy will begin to shifts and eventually lightens up.

You can also create your own request to the universe to help you remove any heavy feelings that you are experiencing.

- *Spend time alone*

One of the best energy balancers is time spent alone. As an empath, you need it constantly. It is a special time to rejuvenate yourself away from others.

Use your time alone wisely and consciously. You can use it to meditate, do yoga, read a book, do something creative, or dance. Once your energy is replenished and balanced, your capacity to love and nurture is greater.

- *Ground yourself with nature*

  Nature provides healing, grounding, and calming effects. Set a regular time for communing with nature.

  Sit under a tree, close your eyes then imagine all the negative energies leaving your body. Another recommended way to ground yourself is to walk barefoot and feel the sensations that the earth's soil gives you.

- *Learn more techniques of energetic cleansing and protection rituals*

Here are other effective ways to protect yourself:

- o Basking in Sunshine or Moonshine
- o Taking a bath with crystals and candles
- o Burning Sage or Essential Oils
- o Digital Detox
- o Practicing gratitude every day
- o Praying
- o Visualizing White Light

Positive affirmations and why they work.

An affirmation is a positive statement that you declare repeatedly to the universe and to yourself. It is meant to motivate you to stay strong against the challenge and overcome negative thoughts.

As you repeat it over and over again, you are planting a positive claim to the result as what you believe. You are sending a positive energy into the universe and you are attracting matched energies that will eventually transform into great manifestations.

Two significant things happen when you utter positive affirmations repeatedly.

First, you are sending a clear message to your Reticular Activating System (RAS) that it is very important to you. RAS is a brain component which filters unnecessary information. It helps the brain register the information that matters based on your goals, interests, desires, and needs. It will also become busy in finding ways to assist you towards achieving your intention or goal.

If money is your goal, there will be earning and investment opportunities that will manifest. If you aim to lose weight, you will become more aware of various weight loss products, gyms, and other ways to attain it.

In short, positive affirmations kick your creativity to the max!

Second, positive affirmations also produce a dynamic tension within you because you are affirming something in a higher vibration. It challenges you to raise the bar to match the affirmation with reality.

- It reprograms your thinking patterns which will eventually alter how you think and act. You become a more positive individual.

- It helps you perform better. Practicing positive affirmation prior to a meeting or presentation can help calm your nerves and boosts your confidence.

- It mitigates the negative effects of stress.

- It aids people who are dealing with depression, low self-esteem, and mental health issues by stimulating brain areas that influence positive changes.

- It increases your feelings of self-worth.

- It spurs you to act and change your old behavior.

- It controls negative feelings like impatience, frustration, or anger.

- It improves your productivity.

- It helps you overcome a bad habit.

- Determine the change or transformation that you want to happen in yourself or in your life.

- Add some words that express emotions to the general statement.

- Make it positive.

Chapter 5
Using Sexual Energy

Sexual energy is quite the potent fuel that you can use to empower your life, in its transmuted energy form. Once transformed, it can become your tool to create, invent, achieve, advance, and accomplish great things.

This life force is settled in the root or sacral chakra located in the base of your spine. It is associated with the reproductive organ. It fuels the entire energy system of the body.

Basically, this energy is used during sex and other pleasurable intentions.

Healing through transmutation and what it is and how to use it.

Transmutation is defined as the transformation of one substance into another form. In the context of empath healing, the sexual transmutation or sexual sublimation is used to facilitate spiritual awakening.

This sexual energy is a potent tool to healing. Transmitting it requires intention.

The most powerful form is when you turn sexual energy into spiritual bliss. This works by consciously moving the sexual energy from your first chakra which is the genital area, up to the higher chakras. This motion will produce an implosion of blissful energy, instead of exploration in the genitals which is the sexual orgasm.

When the transmuted genital energy passes through the next six energy centers or chakras, you will experience an enriching and healing experience which can be mind-blowing. You will see life from a new perspective. You will be transformed. You will feel more connected to the people around you. You will see difficult circumstances in a better light. Even your communication skills are enhanced.

Another technique to transmute sexual orgasm energy into healing energy is to decide where to dedicate it prior to lovemaking. Energy follows your intention. Find someone who needs healing. You can use it to heal Mother Earth.

There are also techniques that use magic rituals, spells, and symbols to transmute the sexual energy into positive affirmations or life actions.

Using this energy and awakening life force.

Sexual energy is part of your life force. You cannot create or destroy it, you can only transform it into a higher form of energy to heal.

Harnessing sexual energy to awaken life force

Step 1: Preparation Stage – Raising Sensuality

To raise the level of your sexual energy, focus your mind on things or activities that excite you, including great sex.

Another way is to practice tantric massage. You will use your hand to move the energy and to accumulate more. At the same time, you are also massaging your body muscles. To start, place your hand just above the skin of your feet. Move your hand slowly from the bottom of your feet, then to your legs and up to your first chakra.

Next, move your hand on top of your arms to the top of your head, then down to the chakras until it reaches the sacral chakra. Imagine the movement and accumulation of energy in each channel of energy as you move your hand. One good thing to remember is to move the sexual energy through your kidneys to enhance cleansing of the body.

Once you reach the sacral chakra, move your hand clockwise in the front and back area of your body. You will sense a warming effect as you focus on increasing your sensuality. At this point, you accumulated a great amount of sexual energy that is ready to be used for healing or manifesting.

Remember that sexual energy equates love energy. When you focus on people or things you love, the results are much quicker.

Step 2: Moving the Accumulated Energy to Your Heart Chakra

Now that you have the accumulated energy at your disposal, you need a container to store it before you begin the healing process. The heart chakra is the best place to store it. You need the expanded heart chakra, meaning the heart, the solar plexus, and the throat chakra. These will become the vessels of your collected energy.

You can also repeat the process of accumulating energy 2-3 times before moving it all to the expanded heart chakra. At this point, all your chakras will be thoroughly activated. Don't worry if there is an overflow of energy when you start moving it to the heart chakra. There is no danger when energy leaks.

To move the energy, guide it using your hand and imagination from the sacral chakra up to the expanded heart chakra. Do not rush the motion, use slow and fluid movements at the front and back of your body.

Step 3: Healing

To use the energy for healing, imagine the result that you want to achieve in your third eye. Picture it in details, including the feelings that are related to complete healing. It is important to empower your intention to heal emotions.

Using your mind, communicate with your cell community in the body and ask it to welcome the healing energy that you will be sending. Express clearly the outcome that you want to achieve as you work with them. Acknowledge your cells' intelligence and cooperation as they accept healing. With your empowered feelings and thoughts, express your love for your body. This is how you send love to your body at the physical level.

Step 4: Continuing the Process

At this point, move the accumulated energy through your pineal gland, the area behind the third chakra and send it directly to the affected or diseased organ. Include your positive emotions, desires, and positive affirmations.

As you do it, you may feel the sensation of orgasm, use it also to send a final massive amount of healing energy.

Step 5: Closing

You used a massive wave of healing energy inside your body. These results in the creation of new transmission pipes where healing energy can flow anytime you want.

At this point, you need to stabilize and balance the energy in your body. It is recommended to use natural ways like meditation or Reiki. Any of these two techniques will dispel all the blocked energies as well as the spent energies that remain inside the body. Releasing them all will make you refreshed and ready for another healing session.

Section 2

17 survival habits for an Empath

Chapter 6
First Step to Survival

The empath's existence is constantly invaded by the energy and emotions of other people, animals, objects, and places. Empaths face each day dealing with minor to major emotional or mental battles that are not their own.

If you are unaware that you are an empath, you might begin to think that you are having deep-seated emotional issues. But when you become more enlightened about your unique characteristics as an empath, it will be easier to survive the drama of everyday life.

As an empath, you are naturally giving. This can be of your time, effort, money, and presence. It is in your nature to help and nurture, to heal and care. But in the long run, all these benevolent acts will actually drain your own strength and life force. It will wear you down to the point of physical illness, emotional stress, and mental fatigue. You must remember to take care of yourself first and stop others from draining your own energy.

This chapter and next chapters will help you cope and survive.

The first step to survival – Identification of Drainers and Energizers

This is the most important step that you need to do if you are an empath. You need to figure out who, what, when, where, and how your energy is being drained. Similarly, knowing your energizers is vital to survival.

Drainers

- *Toxic people-* These "energy vampires" will sap all of your positive energy and leave you spent, tired, and weak.

- *Negative discussions* – Stay away from people who are fond of sharing sad stories. If you find yourself in the midst of a negative discussion, walk away and leave the group to prevent absorbing the overwhelming emotions that are present.

- If you cannot avoid them permanently because these people happen to be close to you—such as your family, your boss, or your best friend, politely tell them to stop relating those kinds of stories. If they don't stop, then they are not respecting your boundaries. It is not rudeness to tell them that you don't want to hear their stories or opinions, it is essential for your well-being and survival.

- *News on TV or Newspapers-* For empaths, reading or watching the news can be a tiring and emotionally draining experience. You easily attach yourself to what you see or hear in the news especially stories that make you teary-eyed.

You feel the pain, fear, sadness, or suffering of victims and you carry these emotions as your own. You are like a sponge who absorbs every heart-breaking story that you see on the screen. You absorb the anger, the frustrations, the hopelessness, and fears of people who are fighting for their own survival. Unconsciously, you are identifying yourself with those people.

- *News feeds on Facebook and other social media channel* – If your news feeds are full of horrible images with shocking stories, stop reading them. Hide them and other related posts so your feed becomes a safe zone for you.

- *Buses, Trains, and Planes* – You are also sensitive in subtle shifts so public transportation usually drains your energy. You cannot stand the hustle and bustle of the crammed crowd. The noise, the bumps, and turns can stress you out.

- *Hospital* – This is a war zone for empaths. Since it is a place where suffering and pain are obvious, you can easily become affected by different negative emotions that seep through every corner of a hospital.

- *Stressful Work Environments* – Working in a hostile environment is another drainer for empaths like you. The negative energy creates tension and stress.

- *Group Therapy Sessions* – They may be therapeutic for others but for empaths, they are energy-drainers. It is best to find a group of empaths who offer support and healing for each other.

- *Traumatic, sad, or violent films* – If you find yourself exhausted, emotionally drained, or have a sick gut feeling after watching movies that belong to these categories, it is best to avoid them.

Energizers

- *Connect with like-minded souls* – Browse online and find groups of empaths that support each other. If you know someone in your local community, join them to be more enlightened.

- *Set clear boundaries* – Limit your time when dealing with emotional situations or people. Let them know that you only have a short period of time to be with them. Do not let them coax, bully, or make you feel guilty about not staying long. You have the choice and you need to be in control of your time and attention. Create a schedule to balance everything.

- *Practice grounding* – Whenever you feel out of control, practice grounding.

  Find a quiet place and take off your shoes. Standing barefoot, touch a tree and visualize roots of lights penetrating your feet like the roots of the tree. Let them absorb all the negative energies inside your body. Release the emotional energies that make you feel out of balance.

Chapter 7
Second Step to Survival

The next most important thing that helps empaths face the daily struggle of living a balanced and healthy life is their energy shield. This protective energy helps keep them from being affected or influenced by different energies that come from people they encounter every day.

Here are some of the most effective ways of shielding:

- **Energetic hygiene shielding**

This involves a daily habit of visualization, meditation, clearing, or grounding techniques. One of them is enough but it will be more beneficial if you can do more than one to enhance your inherent psychic abilities and sustain your positive energy.

Habitual cleansing of energy helps you clearly delineate your own emotions from others' emotions.

- **Sustaining a vibrant physical health**

View yourself as an energy being. Your body emits electrically charged energies like a light bulb or a radio signal. When you are strong, you are more powerful. You radiate a positive and contagious energy that dispels negative energies.

To sustain this energy, you need healthy food, clean water, beneficial exercise, proper rest, adequate sleep, and positive self-talk.

- **Surrounding yourself with a bubbling energy**

Imagine yourself inside a positively charged energy bubble. The bubble protects you from outside energies. When you are protected, you can focus your mind inward and create balance.

Anytime you feel emotionally drained, retreat inside your bubble energy shield and recharge.

- **Visualizing a circle**

Imagine a circle of light around your entire body whenever you need to interact with people during emotional discussions. It is the easiest way to shield you against toxic people and situations.

This circle of light will keep you from becoming aware of anyone's intention or hidden emotion that will affect your clear perspective on the matter. It allows you to be emotionally present, compassionate and grounded, while keeping up with the conversation.

- **Wearing energetically shielding silk fabric**

Silk can neutralize negative energies around a big crowd. It shields you from challenging emotions and vibrations.

Invest in silk garments like dresses, handkerchiefs, shirts, and shawls which can be handy when you need to present in a gathering which you expect a lot of people.

- **Using protective jewelry**

Wearing crystals can protect you from emotional patterns that emit anger, loneliness, or desperation. Use symbolic jewelry that you believe is powerful. Some use little mirrors to set their intention of reflecting back the negativities. Others use turquoise, hematite, or white quartz to ward off unpleasant vibrations.

- **Empathic shielding using Light visualization**

The concept of White Light or Pink Light Shielding helps you invoke spiritual protection, support, and nurturing from the Higher Power.

- White Light – It is the strongest and impermeable shield that you can use.

- Pink Light – It is the aura color that represents your Higher Self. It is ethereal, soft, and tender-hearted protection. It showers you loving energy, compassion, goodwill, and understanding.

  It is a semi-permeable shield but it works as a filter that blocks the psychic attack or emotional contagion and as a mirror that bounces back evil intentions or debilitating energy.

Chapter 8
Protecting Your Intuition and Energy from Others

If you don't own your own energy, others will rob it from you.

This is true. People can be energy vampires and sap your energy if you will not spend it wisely or use it for your own good.

Perhaps, you are spending many years of your life allowing others to sweep you with their energies. You might begin to believe that it is normal or you are doing it to show your compassion, support, or love. For such a long time, you might have also been wondering why you react with negativity when it is not your real nature. This only means that others' negativity has already penetrated your core.

To restore your authentic self, you need to release the negativity and protect your intuition and energy from toxic people. You need to take ownership of your own energy; it is the only way to give the best to the world.

- **Become more aware**

Exercise your intuition by becoming aware of people, places, objects, and situations that surround you. It will strengthen your intuitive power and heightened your awareness. These will keep you sane as you encounter emotional minefields every day.

- **Connect with the rhythm of your own breath**

Negative vibrations or energies can make you lose connection with your breathing. This is characterized by short, shallow breathing or difficulty of breathing when facing a toxic situation or people.

To restore the connection, pull back slowly and become more aware of the rise and fall of your chest as you inhale and exhale. When you inhale, imagine a soft, loving light entering your body. When you exhale, imagine a dark, negative energy leaving your body. Repeat them until you feel your energy is back and you are whole again.

- **Guard yourself**

Establish clear energetic limits or boundaries to detach yourself from the messy energies of people around you.

Before leaving your house, visualize putting a protective cloak over your body or around it. You can also use symbolic objects like a piece of cloth, a white paper or a hat to remind you of the boundary that you set up. Place a strong protective intention in any of these symbols to keep you guarded.

- **Activate the sacred space**

You are special. You are created with a subtle, sacred energy that protects you. You have the sole power to strengthen it and make it works for you. When you activate your sacred space with love and respect, it will do the same for you. Harness and use this space for loving intentions.

The ways to activate it includes taking purifying shower or bath, nurturing the body and space with extra-attention, lighting candles, performing a clearing ritual, or smudging regularly.

- **Turn on your light**

It is only the light that can expunge the darkness, turn it on. Spread a loving energy. Open your heart and stay positive. Do not allow negative emotions like anger, disgust, or frustration enters your system when it comes.

Send soothing pink light to negative people and situations. Spread love using this intention – *"I represent love to wherever I am; therefore I share it with you."*

Chapter 9
How to Maintain Energy

If you often find yourself emotionally, physically, and mentally drained because of work, family, and social obligation, then you need quick recharging strategies that will keep you sustain your healthy energetic state. Facing life with a low level of energy makes you vulnerable against energy vampires.

Here are some simple and quick ways to keep you empowered at all times:

- **Take deep breaths**

This is the simplest method to restore balance to your energy. Your breath is the quickest path to access, rejuvenate, and unlock your power. Regular, deep breaths calm the central nervous system. They relieve tension and emotional problems, support mental clarity, eliminate toxins, improve blood circulation, strengthen lungs, improve posture, and a lot more.

When you feel overloaded with a myriad of energy, anxious, or drained, pause for a while and take life-cleansing breaths. The 8/8/8 method is best for you.

Every morning and anytime you need to, take 8 slow breaths through your nose then out through your mouth, then 8 in through the nose, out through the nose, and culminate it with 8 breathes in and out through your mouth. As you do the breathing, imagine that you are releasing the excess energy from your body and auric field.

- **Still your mind through meditation**

For empaths, the act of stillness is empowering. It is when you allow new life-sustaining energy into your body and mind. You are a vessel that needs to be emptied and re-filled regularly in order to be more receptive and productive.

A daily 5-minute meditation practice will help you find your center and keep your mind still. In silence, you are more empowered. God speaks to you when you are in the state of stillness.

- **Ground in Nature**

Nature offers the fastest and most natural way of boosting your energy. Make it a habit to practice 5-minute grounding by standing barefoot on grass, rocks, and soil.

The act will transmute the negative energy as well as the technology pollution that are stored in your body and release it with the help of the earth's electromagnetic field. This will free your mind from worry, calms your central nervous system, and heals your entire body.

Chapter 10
Negative People's Energy

Like you, other people will also have dominant energies that affect the people around them. Everyone has their own energy fields. You feel the energy clinging to you, following you, or settling in you. Highly sensitive people or empaths can easily recognize these conditions.

The first step is to be aware. Awareness or mindfulness helps you ward off the energy emanating from other people. Become aware of your unique energy signature, your own consciousness, and your ability to tune in to your Higher Self.

Next, be prepared. It requires discipline, conscious, and deliberate action to keep your energy vibrant at all times. This will not only make you more empowered towards stopping negative energy, but it will also make you feel more alive, free, healthy, and happy.

Third, stay away from toxic people who:

- Belittle you in any way.

- Make you feel exhausted or give you physical sensations of chills, upset stomach, palpitations, or pains.

- Attempt to boss or control you.

- Talk non-stop about their problems, themselves, or gossip about others.

- Like sharing morbid or negative stories.

- Try to invade your privacy without your knowledge or pry information from you.

- Rage about people, use profane, ugly, and hate terms.

- Deceive you in any way.

Chapter 11
Positive Affirmation to Heal

Sickness is usually a product of negative thoughts that turn into habits, whether physical, mental, or emotional.

Your mind and body connection work together to keep you healthy, positive, and happy. With a positive outlook, you will begin to radiate higher energy which produces love, joy, and gratitude. But, when you keep negative emotions bottled up inside you, your energy becomes weak. When your energy is low, you are prone to illness.

A healthy, positive mind is one of the best defenses to help beat sickness. To keep it healthy, feed your mind with positive affirmations that will heal and strengthen your body, mind, and spirit.

Here are some of the most effective positive affirmations:

1. I choose to heal my body, soul, mind, and heart every day.

2. My body is healthy. My mind is brilliant. My soul is at peace.

3. Each cell in my body is vibrating with health and energy.

4. I forgive myself and I forgive those who hurt me.

5. I manifest excellent health in spirit, body, and mind.

6. I am thankful for the healing process that is happening right now inside my body, mind, and spirit.

7. I am beautiful, strong, radiant, and healthy.

8. I give permission for my body to be healed inside and out.

9. I am healing in my time.

Your thoughts create your own reality. If you think positive, you will attract positive results.

Chapter 12

How to Cut Down & Block Negative Energy?

Almost everyone seeks to live a more peaceful life. However, there are many negative influences in our surroundings that will try to stop us from achieving this objective. And not all of these negative energies comes from the outside. Some are from within you like bad habits. All these negative influences put dents in your self-confidence, happiness, and productivity.

Here are some steps to block negative energy and live more positively:

- **Remove the toxic people**

Spend less time or totally avoid friends or colleagues who gossip about you or relatives that always ridicule or criticize you. Do not obsess on what they say about you. Say goodbye to them.

- **Choose to be with positive people**

If you cannot altogether remove some people out of your life, mingle with positive people to balance the energy.

- **Go offline**

If social media is making you feel depressed with so many negative news and images that are posted, stop checking it constantly. Detach yourself from the virtual world and begin to live consciously in your real surroundings.

- **Declutter**

A cluttered space also clutters your mind. Too many possessions, trinkets, and souvenirs can make you exhausted because it takes up lots of time to keep them clean.

Get rid of junk and things that you do use anymore. Donate your old clothes.

- **Do not entertain self-doubt**

Be confident. Take charge of your life. Stop over thinking because it leads to self-doubt.

Tear down the barrier of doubts that hinder you from achieving all your goals and dreams.

Chapter 13
Healing Mind, Body, and Soul

People. Feelings. Energy. Sensations. Words. Pain. Anger.

All these can affect an empath overwhelmingly. They can make you feel sick to the core. You can pick them up unconsciously and feel them as if they were your own. Thus, the importance of recognizing and shielding yourself constantly. If you feel that you have excessive energy inside you, it's time to heal your mind, body, and soul to prevent illness.

Exercising all aspects of Life

Life is not always going to be all sunshine, especially if you are an empath. You will always be influenced by the energy of others who can deplete your own energy. To help and heal yourself, you need to exercise caution in all aspects of your life.

- **Control Your Mind**

Your thoughts are your own responsibility. Over thinking or thinking negatively can only aggravate your situation and make you sick. Healing can only set in if you accept the situation. Change your thinking and stop resisting to gain a better result.

- **Practice Visualization**

Visualization is a magnificent mind tool that heals the mind, body, and spirit. When visualizing, see yourself as a healthy and robust person. Do not allow negativity. Stay joyous and positive.

- **Have a strong faith and belief**

Never allow yourself to wallow in moments of doubt. Practice positive thinking. Be with positive people that you love. Surround yourself with books, videos, and other materials about mind body spirit healing. Begin your day with positive affirmation to anchor your belief and faith.

- **Learn to Mindfully Relax**

Find relaxation techniques that can help you alleviate stress and strengthen the immune system.

- **Release Resentment**

Forgive and forget. Anger and resentment can negatively affect your well-being and health. Forgive yourself and people who harm you.

- **Live in Gratitude**

Every day, find one or more things that make you feel grateful. Give thanks to God, to people, and even to yourself. This will raise your consciousness and make you the center of the divine blessings.

Chapter 14
Blocking Negative Energies as They Come

If you can block negative energy as soon they come or even before they hit you, then all the better. Here are some effective blocking ways:

- **Shielding**

Keep your doors of energy closed. Your personal energy space must always be free from negative energy. Do not allow other people to enter your field of energy. Stop giving them an opportunity to influence or affect your balance.

- **Detaching**

To prevent being drained, distance yourself from negative people. Stay away from friends or co-workers who talk incessantly about their feelings or problems.

Excuse yourself politely during the conversation or find an excuse to end the conversation.

- **Using Crystals**

Crystals and stones provide protection and transmute energy. For protection, choose Turquoise, Amethyst, Black Onyx, Emerald, Hematite, and Obsidian. They can deflect negative energies. You can keep it in your pocket, put it on your desk, sleep near it, or wear it as an accessory.

Chapter 15
Being Selective Whom You Hang Out With

Being selective with who you spend time with is also a form of self-care. The type of people who keep you company can impact your life especially because you are an empath.

Negativity is contagious so you need to take extra care when choosing who you keep for life. Fill your life with people who genuinely care for you, celebrate with you during happy moments, support you when you are at your lows, and motivate you to become a better version of yourself.

Say goodbye to toxic people, who love drama and gossip.

How do choose friends?

- *Choose friends who stretch you*

They are people with purpose. They are uplifting, positive, encouraging, and motivating.

- *Choose friends who bring balance*

The right friends will tap your talents, abilities, and skills. You utilize each other's strengths and helps to overcome weaknesses.

- *Choose friends with common life goals*

Call them your purpose partners. With common goals, you push each other to achieve success. You even work together or collaborate on projects.

Chapter 16
How to Maintain a Positive Outlook?

One of the challenges that an empath face is maintaining a positive mindset because of your susceptibility to absorbing negative energy around you. You need to recognize your own emotions as well as others' emotions and create a separation.

During tough times, it is necessary to strike a balance by not suppressing their emotions especially negative ones and focusing on the brighter sides of life.

Tips to Maintain Positivity:

- *Acknowledge your emotions*

Do not be afraid to face your emotions- anger, frustration, sadness, resentment, and other unpleasant feelings. People used to bury them deep down inside because they are detrimental.

However, when you hide them inside, they become like wounds which remain unhealed.

On the other hand, when you express them as they come, you are processing them and soon they lose their power over you.

- *Focus on positivity*

After allowing yourself to be upset while facing and processing your emotion, you can now focus on the next step with a clearer mind-focusing on the good stuff.

Create a gratitude journal and write things that make you thankful. Add at least 3 things every day. You will soon realize that life is good.

Review your past achievements. You already achieved a lot of your goals, do not be discouraged because of a minor setback.

You have people who love you and support you. When you focus on them, you shift your focus from negativity to positivity. You will better.

- *Have fun every day*

Make a commitment to try and add more fun to what you do daily. It is something that you will look forward to as you wake up in the morning and keeps you from staying on the negative side of life.

It can be anything from hanging out with good friends, watching your favorite TV show, listening to music, or reading a new book. Schedule a specific time to do it.

Chapter 17
NLP Reframe for Joy

NLP or Neuro-Linguistic Programming is a powerful technique to help you change your behavior and how you experience life. It can literally transform your whole existence. It provides several happiness strategies that make you live a more meaningful and joyous life.

- Anchoring

This works by associating a positive emotion or thought to an anchor which can be in the form of gesture, word, or gesture. It can elicit an immediate positive response and keeps you in control of your feelings.

Anchoring is similar to the concept of conditioning. The stimulus triggers response through repetition.

- Reframing of Content

It is the concept of viewing event or situation from another frame of perspective. Reframing helps you see positive possibilities instead of dwelling on the negative.

- **Belief–Changing**

When you reframe, it reduces any of the self-limiting beliefs that you form. For more established beliefs, you need to gain more facts to help you change your limiting beliefs and affirm it daily until it becomes part of your consciousness.

- **Disassociating**

NLP helps you disassociate from a negative situation or person by diffusing the heightened emotions and restoring your objectivity.

Chapter 18
Releasing Negative Thoughts and Emotions

It is a necessity for empaths to maintain their energy fields clear from negative emotions and thoughts. This will help keep them grounded and centered.

Use of Crystals

Crystals can help you repeal negative energies. You can wear it or put it inside your purse or pocket.

Black Tourmaline

It is a powerful repelling stone. Place it in the entrance of your home to dispel incoming negative energy. It can also be placed in the center of your home in order to radiate negative energy outward.

Apache Tears Obsidian

They are small, black glass nodules that originated from the domes and lava flows. These semi-translucent stones release negative energy and heal lower emotions such as grief, mourning, or sadness.

Tiger's Eye

They keep you grounded and protected amidst negative energy. They provide calmness and clarity even if you are surrounded by lower thoughts and emotions. No matter the situation, you can be able to make clear decisions.

Chapter 19
How to Find More Joy in Life?

You are a sensitive soul. You are special. Your high sensitivity to energy can be a good or negative thing for you. As an empath, you can be emotional, drained, and tired most of the day because of the swirling emotions of other people. Most of the time, you feel sad and lonely even if there is no reason to.

Improve your life. Guard yourself against unhappiness. Find more joy.

- **Express Gratitude**

Gratitude is more than just the act of saying thank you. It is about cultivating an appreciation for what you have right now and what is around you.

Don't take the people who have your best interest in their hearts for granted. Stop the non-stop wants and needs as most of these are unnecessary and only cause you stress.

- **Find Your Purpose**

What excites you most? The answer can lead you to your purpose in life. Purpose-driven individuals are happier and healthier.

Find out something that you are passionate about and pursue this goal. This will increase your energy and enthusiasm.

- **Enhance Your Relationships**

Take care of your relationships- marital, friendship, family, and other important affairs. Invest in your relationship and you will be greatly rewarded.

- **Engage**

Do things that make you happy. Listen to music. Sing and dance. Take a break and have a vacation. Travel. Find new places to eat. Start your hobby.

Chapter 20
How to Stay More Positive and Productive with Energy?

Since you already know that you are an empath and have a better understanding of what that entails, then you also are more equipped when it comes to dealing with it.

Here are more ways to help you productive and positive:

- **Pull away**

Detach yourself from negativity. You can sense it right away as you enter a room or meet a person. Steer clear from arguments, emotional moments, and crowds. They can make you unproductive and emotionally vulnerable.

Pull away as soon as you sense it and shield yourself.

- **Power up**

Exercise, meditate, practice yoga, and do something you love. This will fill you up with energy as well as help you release excess energy.

- **Write**

Making journals is a wonderful energy neutralizer. Buy a new journal and record your innermost feelings. Release your negative emotions and express your overwhelming excitement to prevent energy overload. Besides, handwriting your experiences seems to be more healing and soothing.

- **Water Therapy**

Water helps you stay hydrated and flushes out any unwanted energy. Drink lots of water.

Take a cool shower or a hot shower, whichever you feel best to wash the energies that are attached to your own energy space.

- **Sleep it away**

A good night sleep allows your body, mind, and soul to rest. You will wake up invigorated and refreshed.

Chapter 21
Understanding Who to Let in Your Circle

Your sensitivity can lure in a lot of people who want someone to listen, to understand, and to care for them. You are that kind of person because you genuinely care for others. However, because of your empathic gifts, you can also become the target of emotional vampires who will drain your energy and leave you emotionally drained.

Be wise when it comes to who you allow in your circle with these vital questions:

- What do they add to your life?

- Why would you let them in?

You need to avoid letting in people who make you feel the following sensations:

- Fatigue – You feel a sudden tiredness. If they are venting, you struggle to stop yourself from yawning or closing your eyes.

- Anger – While you are with the person, there is a feeling of bitterness that creeps into you. It can last up to 10 days if you do not know how to release negative energy.

- Judgmental behavior – Extremely toxic people can make you judgmental of others even though it is not your normal nature. They can influence you to talk negatively about people.

- Apathy- They makes you lose your optimism and zest.

- Strange feelings- It includes nausea, headaches, or being spaced out.

Chapter 22

Reasons to Recharge- Why and How?

Trapped and unreleased heavy emotions inside of your body can make you sick, weak, and restless. As an empath, you will need to release them in order to prevent an energy overload. If you do not detoxify yourself, this can lead to damaging physical, mental, and emotional issues.

How do empaths recharge?

By making a choice. Your choice is imperative to your well-being and survival. You need to embrace your unique gift and personality. Then, train your mind to focus on positive energy.

Seek nature. It is a great rejuvenator of energy.

Be creative. When you express your talent and creativity, you channel your energy into a positive purpose.

Take care of your physical body. Practice mindful eating, exercise regularly and meditate to center your energy.

Ground as often as you can to sustain a healthy, positive energy.

Conclusion

Thank you for reading this book **Empath: Why Your Intuition Matter and What's Your Body is Telling You.**

I hope that I have imparted the gist of essential things that you need to know about an empath life. I know that it is difficult to be one but the fact that you have a special gift is also an exciting thought.

All the chapters are written with the purpose of making life easier for you as you interact with people, situations, and objects that emit strong vibrations. There are tips and strategies in every chapter to make your empath journey stress-free as much as possible.

As an empath, you are a spiritual warrior. You just need to tap your inherent power and learn to level up your own energy.

The 17 survival habits that are listed in section two of the book will help you survive with flying colors.

Own your power by using your intuition and live a happier, healthier, and more meaningful life as an empath.

68292772R00053

Made in the USA
Middletown, DE
15 September 2019